SMALL PRAYERS
FOR
SMALL CHILDREN
about
big and little things

written by PAUL A. SCHREIVOGEL
illustrated by George Ellen Holmgren csj

AUGSBURG PUBLISHING HOUSE
MINNEAPOLIS   MINNESOTA

FOR

JOHN DAVID
CAROL ANNE
and... STEPHAN PAUL

SMALL PRAYERS FOR SMALL CHILDREN

Copyright © 1971 Augsburg Publishing House

Library of Congress Catalog Card No. 76-135226
International Standard Book No. 0-8066-1109-X

Manufactured in the United States of America

This is a talking book, with pictures and words to help parents
and small children talk about the small and big things of life.
This book is not the end of prayers, but the beginning.
You can supplement it with the rich traditional prayers of the
past and your own new prayers.

The style of these prayers is talking and seeing, not reciting.
Hopefully, the words will point to the pictures, and the pictures
to the words, and both pictures and words to the life of the child.

PAUL A. SCHREIVOGEL
George Ellen Holmgren CSJ

MORNING

LET MY EYES SEE
    GOOD THINGS TODAY.
LET MY MOUTH TALK
    HAPPY TODAY.
LET MY EARS LISTEN
    WELL TODAY.
LET ME ENJOY TODAY.

after a MEAL

Thank you for this good meal, LORD, and bless Mother, who must now wash the DISHES.

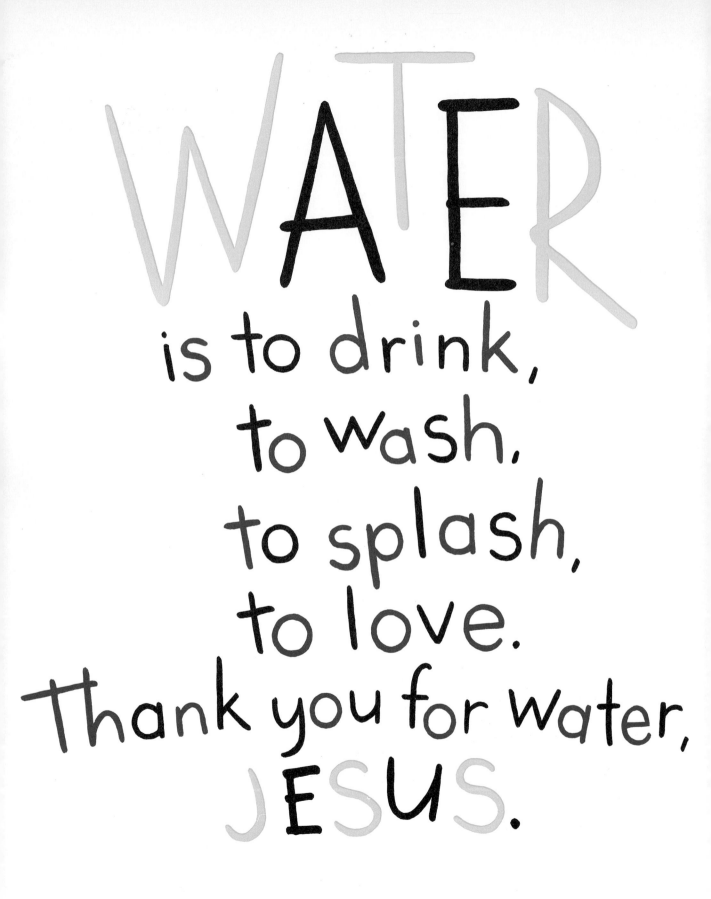

WATER
is to drink,
to wash,
to splash,
to love.
Thank you for water,
JESUS.

WORDS ARE FUN, GOD.
MUD, SUN, JESUS, BLUE,
MOM, EAT, PRAY, NAP,
WORK, PLAY, TABLE, CHAIR,
TV, BOOK, GAMES, LIGHT,
TOYS, DARK.

THANK YOU for words like
LOVE, LOVE,
LOVE, LOVE.

sounds

SOUNDS
are beautiful,
FATHER.
The honk-honk of cars.
THE zoom-zoom of jets.
The beep-beep of buses.
THE drip-drip of water.
The splash-splash
of puddles.
AND THE SOUNDS OF
PEOPLE LAUGHING.

FRIENDS

O HOLY SPIRIT

MY FRIEND
PUSHED ME DOWN
AND I DIDN'T DO
ANYTHING.

Oh. I get so·ooooo mad.
Help him not to be so pushy
AND ME NOT GET
        S·O·OOOO MAD.

MOON

BEAUTIFUL JESUS

who visit the MOON

THE MOON IS BEAUTIFUL.
Bless the moon.
Bless the people who visit the moon.
Bless all the moons,
and stars and skies.
BLESS, O JESUS,
all things
UP HIGH.

THINGS

Thank you, heavenly FATHER,
for trees and twigs,
for buildings and bricks,
for streets and walks,
for land and grass,
AND FOR ALL THINGS I CAN
SEE, TOUCH, AND HEAR.

fall

FOR PUMPKINS
and Charlie Brown,
for THANKSGIVING and turkeys
for bright leaves and crisp air,
for happiness and peace,
for all this and MORE,
THANK YOU
LORD.

winter

THE AIR IS COLD,
we play in the snow,
we sing Christmas songs,
I LIKE WINTER.

REMIND ME, JESUS,
TO PUT ON MY BOOTS,
so I don't catch
COLD.

SHAPES

FOR ROUND CIRCLES and
SQUARE SQUARES,
FOR THREE SIDED TRIANGLES
and SIX SIDED BLOCKS,
FOR ALL ODD THINGS
with no corners and no sides,
I PRAISE YOU, LORD.

LORD
MY PARENTS are sometimes
NICE,
ANGRY,
happy
silly,
JOYFUL.
They are so good
to have around.

TIME

10 9 8 7 6 5 4 3 11

Get-up time,
  breakfast time,
play time,
  lunch time
nap time, dinner time,
  family time, bed time,
SO MANY KINDS of "can't see time"
"can't touch time" "tick-tock time"
THANK YOU, GOD,
  for all kinds of time.

sick people

O LORD,
I'm sad:
blind people
can't see

deaf people
can't hear

sad people
can't laugh.

HELP the BLIND SEE,
HELP the DEAF HEAR,
HELP the SAD LAUGH.

NIGHT

It has been a fun day, LORD.
Now it is night.
The dark is beautiful.
Give me a good sleep,
LORD.

bad times

LORD,

sometimes
I do bad things.
I don't let friends
play with my toys
I am not fair
with other kids.
I cry when I don't
get my way.
LORD, help me
to be GOOD,
KIND,
LOVING.

IT'S FUN TALKING
TO YOU, GOD
about me
and about JESUS
about your LOVE
and my LOVE
about PEOPLE and THINGS
and how I feel.
IT'S FUN TALKING
TO YOU, GOD.